THE NEW CENTURY

THE NEW CENTURY

POEMS

EWA LIPSKA

TRANSLATED FROM THE POLISH BY
ROBIN DAVIDSON AND
EWA ELŻBIETA NOWAKOWSKA

NORTHWESTERN UNIVERSITY PRESS

EVANSTON, ILLINOIS

Northwestern University Press
www.nupress.northwestern.edu

INSTYTUT KSIĄŻKI

©POLAND

This book has been funded by the Book Institute © POLAND
Translation Program.

The poems were originally published in Kraków by Wydawnictwo Literackie in
the following collections: *1999 (1999), Sklepy zoologiczne (Pet Shops), Ja (I),
Gdzie indziej (Elsewhere), Drzazga (Splinter),* and *Pomarańcza Newtona (Newton's
Orange),* copyright © 1999, 2001, 2003, 2005, 2006, and 2007, respectively,
by Ewa Lipska.

Printed in the United States of America

10   9   8   7   6   5   4   3   2   1

Library of Congress Cataloging-in-Publication Data

Lipska, Ewa.
    [Poems. English. Selections]
    The new century : poems / Ewa Lipska ; translated from the Polish by Robin
Davidson and Ewa Elżbieta Nowakowska.
    p. cm.
    Includes bibliographical references.
    ISBN 978-0-8101-2633-6 (pbk. : alk. paper) 1. Lipska, Ewa—Translations
into English. I. Davidson, Robin, 1953— II. Nowakowska, Ewa Elżbieta,
1972— III. Title.
PG7171.I63A613 2009
891.8517—dc22

                                                  2009024601

In memory of

Simon Wiesenthal

(1908 – 2005)

Contents

THE NEW CENTURY

from **1999** (1999)

Preface: The Absurdity of Beauty

Ewa Lipska

Nietzsche believed that "an artist hates reality." Above all, however, he is its slave and sometimes its victim. Reality repeatedly turns into a trap for us. Unexpectedly and cunningly, we are involved in a spectacle that our lives become.

A few years ago, on a September day, in a small German town something happened that takes us far beyond explainable coincidence and becomes for a writer an inconvenient metaphor, a nagging unrest, an inescapable prison of preposterous speculations and presumptions. I shall not mention the name of the town as it does not affect the violently unfolding action. Pale-pink clouds, the props from a suburban theater, were lingering sluggishly on the roofs of nearby houses. It was getting on toward five o'clock, the time when the world's colors are most daring and obsessive. At first glance you could see a bridge. The bridge, so to speak, suspended by philologists and belles-lettres connoisseurs. It resembled an essay on the architectural structures of language and colloquialisms. Arched, reinforced, with firm spans. As it probably evoked no nostalgia, it did not attract suicides or lovers. Still waves of the Rhine calmly flowed under its massive and neat construction. Near the forest you could see from the bridge a flock

From Ewa Lipska, Sekwens [Sequence] *(Warsaw: Świat Książki, 2003). Translated by Robin Davidson and Ewa Elżbieta Nowakowska. Preliminary translation by Iza Jarosz and Michał Choiński, graduates of the Institute of English Philology, Jagiellonian University, Kraków, Poland, 2004.*

of black sheep grazing on a green canvas of a meadow, the only witnesses of the imminent events. A girl of about twenty, with a bouquet of heather, was walking down the path toward the bridge. As if on cue at that particular hour, she was an ornament of the desolate landscape. She had just stepped beyond the frame's view when she heard the bang. She turned around quickly, and I remember the heather falling out of her hands. It seemed that this sudden burst of a storm, which did not exist, seized us simultaneously with its thunder and lightning and then died away as suddenly as it had appeared.

The event was witnessed by a driver, whose truck was labeled with a green clover: "Wir wünschen viel Glück mit unserem echten vierblättrigen Kleeblatt" (We wish you much luck with our genuine fourleaf clover). A car driving just ahead of him, a gray Volkswagen Passat, took off from the lane and began heading, as if fully consciously, toward the railing of the bridge. The blow met resistance, the railing bent imperceptibly. Finally, it yielded to the pressure, bowed in humiliation, like grass in the wind, and the car tumbled down into the water from a height of a few meters. The truck driver recalls: the gray Volkswagen pulled in front of him just before driving onto the bridge; yes, he saw them perfectly well, a young couple gazing into the flawlessly sketched air. In order to adjust themselves to the facts, the events were artificially constructing the plot; yet, as it turned out later, the facts remained unexplained. The truck driver thought for a moment that the Volkswagen froze in the air, as if changing its mind and deciding to go back or remain in that state of indecision forever. Yet, it plunged into the Rhine. You could hear the roar of the water opening, inviting, *do come in,* as if someone quickly opened the door, not caring about the consequences, and slammed it. In vain. Things conjoined irrevocably, a terror of fate and coincidence, a dictatorship of the moment. A minute later air bubbles, a gurgle, almost as if nothing had happened. A Sunday issue of *Die Zeit, Frankfurter Allgemeine Zeitung* came to the surface of the water. The truck driver was attracted by the deformed letters bending in all possible directions under the transparent surface of the water, drifting away further and further, news washed away by the current.

New things appeared continuously on the water's surface: a white sail of a towel, rafts of pencils, obituaries of notes, all as if trying to escape from the scene of the accident. Then the truck driver heard the scream. He turned around and saw the flock of black sheep, which from now on will be a bad omen for him, woolly symbols of disaster, then he noticed the scattered heather and the screaming girl. "Stop, please . . ." he cried, but half-conscious she looked at him and started running toward the town. Three cars, which he unsuccessfully tried to stop, drove past. The beauty of the setting day intensified and looked like a postcard from a pleasant holiday with an obtrusive perfection of the landscape. More and more items appeared on the surface of the water. They seemed to form a colorful procession of useless things doomed to eternal oblivion. A dead gallery in a liquid peep show. The people from the town were already coming, the cars pulling over and the police and ambulances approaching; it was getting crowded, lights were being turned on. The girl was walking away, abandoning the place forever, first slowly, to avoid suspicion, then fast, very fast, though no one paid any attention to her; she was running, removing the scraps of heather. How did they get in her hair? The black sheep stood still, then blended into the oncoming dusk; they were bequeathed to the event going by forever.

May a poet take advantage of fate in such a situation and describe everything that took place so unexpectedly and suddenly? May he or she dictate to a typist the defenseless facts, add some details, empathize with the victim? To die on a sheet of paper playing the main part, at the same time avoiding compassion that leads to the inevitable corrosion of words? Whom to be in such a situation? An onlooker, a stray wanderer, an agitator? Can you hear the fear and uncertainty when I bend my head over a sheet of paper? Is it pride or humility? The bold consciousness of having something to add, only a few astonished words . . .

From the report of the police officer, Hans Seidler: No irregularities detected. The technical condition of the car very good. Speed limit observed. Suicide excluded. The investigation discontinued.

From the diary of one of the victims:

A forgotten image of childhood: raspberries. A mugful of raspberries. A sweltering summer. I'm running downhill heading for home, the Wienfried pension run by a fat woman whom I used to call "Equator" because she was over forty thousand kilometers around the hips. I was running, maybe even soaring over the ground of colorful squares, tufts of grass, burning stones under my feet. And then, in my path, as if on a hot pan of limestone, next to a silent quarry I saw a coiled adder with a flat, heart-shaped head, distinctly different from the rest of its body. Maybe the head was even separated from the body and returned to it only from time to time. Horrified, I threw the whole mugful of raspberries at the snake and covered it with a hail of pinkish-red fruit. The high fever of this event paralyzed me so completely that I gasped for air with difficulty and could hear my heart pounding. Suddenly awakened, the adder reacted immediately. It drew itself up, jumped like a spring. At first I saw its head, the eyes of the music and mathematics teacher. This image comes upon me always when I lie sleepless. After many years it became mild, slow; my adder has gotten older, it has grown tired. I don't run away anymore like I did that time when the earth, the black backs of serpents, the swampy bogs came apart before me. When I got to the yard, the nurse cried, "Großer Gott, what's happened?" No one was able to help me, it was too late. My life afterward became flammable. I fell in love with women and men. I used to hang out for hours in art galleries and museums. Sometimes I stayed there for nights, months, years. I was dying on the cross and being resurrected in paintings by Piero della Francesca. In the National Gallery in London I fed the Arnolfinis' dog in the painting by Jan van Eyck. In that gallery, looking at the triumph of time over love in Angelo Bronzino's painting, I experienced obscure bliss. In Munich I was shocked by an allegorical figure by Hans Baldung Grien, a naked girl standing on a snake,

treading on it, trampling my whole childhood. I had a terrible fit
of the shivers and had to be walked out of the gallery. I lay for four
days with a high fever in the Land of Sloth, by Pieter Brueghel, only
then to perish in the inferno of Hieronymus Bosch. I was as intimate
with the Garden of Earthly Delights as with life. Then I fell in love
with Rosso's Moses and spent whole days in the gallery in Florence.

Nietzsche thought that "an artist hates reality." Above all, however, he is its slave and sometimes its victim. The boundaries of the soul and the boundaries of countries do not overlap. Decorators improve the landscape, shift furniture, carpets, and numismatic collections. The twentieth century, the century of crime and the triumph of science, is coming to an end. On the great clearing of freedom one may eat hot dogs tasting of an afternoon gutter paper. In the very heart of Vienna, on the wall of the Votivkirche, hangs a huge advertisement: "Mehr Bank, Mehr Chancen, Bank Austria" . . . There is no end of history, there is no end of poetry, new hunters set out; life, like an incurable phrase, bids us welcomes and farewells, the absurdity of beauty will continue to amaze us.

Translators' Acknowledgments

The New Century has emerged from a five-year collaboration, and many generous poets, translators, editors, and scholars have helped us bring this translation project to fruition. We would like to thank, first and foremost, Ewa Lipska for her friendship, the pleasure and brilliance of her poems, and for her invaluable collaboration, year by year, in rendering the selections here into English. We wish to thank Adam Zagajewski—without whom this project might never have been undertaken—for his insights into Polish poetry, culture, and history, and for his ongoing support as friend and teacher. We are also grateful to Wisława Szymborska for her contribution to this volume—*dziękujemy Pani bardzo!* We thank the editors who published early versions of these poems: Sarah Spence, of *Literary Imagination;* Sven Birkerts, of *AGNI;* Natasa Durovicova, of *91st Meridian;* Mira Rosenthal, of *Lyric Poetry Review;* and especially Susan Harris, of *Words Without Borders.* We are also grateful to Bill Martin of the Polish Cultural Institute in New York, whose generosity in connecting us with editors has spanned the duration of the project. In particular, we are indebted to Bill Johnston for his close reading of the original manuscript, his insights into the craft of translation, and his support throughout the publication process.

We are also grateful to the Book Institute of Poland (Instytut Książki) and the National Endowment for the Arts for their support in the development and publication of these translations. Thanks also go to our friends and colleagues at the Institute of English Philology, Jagiellonian University, Kraków, particularly the faculty of the History of British and American Literatures; the faculty of Theoretical Linguistics, Pragmatics, and Translation Theory; and the faculty of Applied Linguistics, and graduates Michał Choiński and Iza Jarosz Choiński. Their generosity over the past five years has been invaluable. And we are indebted to the Fulbright programs in both the United States and Poland for making this international collaboration possible, especially to Dr. Muriel Joffe, of the Council for the International Exchange of Scholars, and Andrzej Dakowski and Dorota Rogowska, of the Polish-U.S. Fulbright Commission.

We also appreciate the support of the University of Houston-Downtown, especially Dr. Susan Ahern, dean of the College of Humanities and Social Sciences, and Dr. William Gilbert, former chair of the Department of English, for their faith in, and ongoing support of, this project. Genuine thanks also go to the many colleagues in the Department of English who generously read and critiqued portions of the translations and introductory prose, and to Robin Reagler and her staff in the Writers in the Schools (WITS) program for the solitude of the WITS House in Houston, where the final versions of these translations were completed.

We are indebted to our families for their patience and support—Ula Nowakowska, Tony Davidson, Joshua Davidson, and Chelsea Davidson—whose presence in our lives deepens the meaning of our work in poetry. Our heartfelt love and thanks to each of you.

And very special thanks go to all those at Northwestern University Press whose commitment to this book have made the publication process a pleasure, especially Anne Gendler, Mike Ashby, Marianne Jankowski, Rudy Faust, and Jenny Gavacs. We are particularly grateful to our editor, Mike Levine, for his enthusiastic appreciation of Lipska's poems early on, and his faith in our translations of them. Thank you, Mike, and all at Northwestern for your superb collaborative spirit.

We would also like to thank the following American literary print and online periodicals, in which seventeen of our poem translations were originally published, between 2003 and 2007. The translations included in this volume, revised since their initial publication, may differ from the previously published versions listed below.

AGNI: "God Asks"

The Bayou Review: "Memory," "That"

Literary Imagination: "December 31, 1991," "No One"

Lyric Poetry Review: "The Accident," "Watch Your Step"

91st Meridian: "The Abyss," "Helplessness," "Plum Cake," "September 11, 2001"

Quarterly West: "When a Great Poet Dies in My Country"

Words Without Borders: "A Juicer," "The New Century," "Number One," "The Smells of Evil," "Splinter"

Art is not always a cure. Sometimes it is poison.
The choice between these two lies within us,
and it is solely up to us whether we will let
a barbaric surge swallow us, or we will
decide to talk with one another.
Let the stars of tolerance be favorable to us.
—Ewa Lipska (translated by Ewa Elżbieta Nowakowska)

Introduction

Robin Davidson

Above the doorframe between the entry hall and the living room of
Ewa Lipska's second-floor flat in Kraków, Poland, a collection of keys
is carefully arranged on tiny nails, a collection I have considered on
many occasions since my first meeting with Lipska and Ewa Nowa-
kowska one brisk January morning in 2004. When asked about the
keys, Lipska simply replied, "I collect them. They are from every-
where." I am reminded of something Walter Benjamin said in his
essay "Unpacking My Library": "Thus there is in the life of the col-
lector a dialectical tension between the poles of order and disorder.
Naturally, his existence is tied . . . to a relationship to objects which
does not emphasize their functional, utilitarian value . . . but stud-
ies and loves them as the scene, the stage, of their fate" (60). I take
Lipska's seemingly offhand remark, much like Benjamin's reflection,
as a comment on the domain of the poet; that is, keys signal meta-
phorically the role of the poet as both riddle maker and truth seeker;
each poem, a system of both secrets and revelations. The translation
of Lipska's poems—built as they are upon wordplay, punning in the

poet's native language—is the task of entry into a mysterious text doubly resistant to being read. It is daunting work. Lipska herself sees the translator's task as heroic, for she asserts that it is translators who sustain an author's existence over time. The very nature of language, unlike music, requires this delicate tightrope dance between author and translator, between one language and another, between sign and meaning. Thus, Nowakowska and I came to the poet's door, to an apartment whose interior walls are built alternately of glass and of bookcases, to find entry into the crystalline, richly ironic poems of a woman who has lived through much of the twentieth century in a nation whose history is one of occupations: German Nazism, Soviet communism, and most recently the increasing presence of American and western European capitalism, what Clare Cavanagh has called the colonization of the Second World (83), or "Coca-Colonialization," as Polish university students are often fond of saying.

Since 1967, Ewa Lipska has published nineteen volumes of poetry, and nearly a book a year since 1996. Her poems have been translated into German, English, French, Dutch, Czech, Slovak, Hungarian, Bulgarian, Albanian, Serbian, Swedish, Danish, Greek, Spanish, and Hebrew. Without the work of translators Barbara Plebanek and Tony Howard, I might never have been able to read Lipska's poems, which I first encountered in English translation in a modern thought class taught by my friend and mentor, Adam Zagajewski, as part of my study of creative writing at the University of Houston. That class prompted in me a wish to learn Polish well enough to read the poems in the original. It was not until the summer of 2001, when Lipska sent me, at Zagajewski's request, a copy of her book *1999,* that I longed to translate these poems myself. With the help of Ewa Nowakowska, to whom Lipska introduced me, that has become possible. *The New Century* begins with fifteen of the twenty poems making up *1999* and includes a total of fifty-nine poems selected from six volumes: *1999* (1999), *Pet Shops* (2001), *I* (2003), *Elsewhere* (2005), *Splinter* (2006), and *Newton's Orange* (2007). These particular works were chosen to illuminate the growth of Lipska's poetic imagination since 1998, when she left the diplomatic position of director of the Polish Institute in Vienna, her home for seven years and a city she still frequents and loves. They offer a deeply private and personal vision framed by European and Jewish history and articulating a struggle against the forces of evil—their reasoned, systematic violence. This vision has developed, in part, from Lipska's deep friendships with Nobel laureate Wisława Szymborska and Holocaust survivor Simon Wiesenthal.

Born in 1945, in Kraków, Ewa Lipska was one of the first poets born in the Polish People's Republic. Like Adam Zagajewski and Stanisław Barańczak, she is among those Polish poets who followed two significant twentieth-century generations, first that of Aleksander Wat, Anna Swirszczyńska, and Czesław Miłosz, born between 1900 and 1911, and second that of Krzysztof Baczyński, Tadeusz Różewicz, Wisława Szymborska, and Zbigniew Herbert, born in the 1920s. Lipska has been described by some as one of the Nowa Fala, or New Wave poets, the younger generation of writers who led a democratic movement in Poland in the late 1960s. Ironically, neither Zagajewski, who was an activist in the 1968 political movement, nor Lipska herself consider her among the Generation of '68. She sees her work as emerging from an individuality unaffiliated with any group or school. Although her poems are at times deeply concerned with the events of World War II and have a rich political and historical consciousness, she is interested primarily in the fate of the individual without regard to national boundaries. She writes in her preface to our translation, "The boundaries of the soul and the boundaries of countries do not overlap."

Lipska's rejection of nationalism is consistent with her vision of the artist's role in society. She would argue that the poet does not craft a work out of sheer will or calculation; rather, art depends on an innocence rooted in a fidelity to personal experience, an authentic response to one's life that is lost in politics, or any other highly organized, artificial social system. The solidarity of poets, unlike that of political regimes, or of activists organized against them, is not a matter of design. Poetry is not collective life. It arises from solitude; it cannot be planned. Lipska thinks of art not only as a rejection of political intention but also as a deliberate engagement with the irrational and with uselessness. When Benjamin says that the collector is not interested in objects for their utilitarian value but instead "loves them as the scene, the stage, of their fate," he could have as easily attributed this tendency to the artist whom Lipska envisions when she writes, "There are no poets. / There is only the inattentive moment."

Lipska was educated as a painter at the Academy of Fine Arts in Kraków, and her *ars poetica* is informed by twentieth-century artistic movements in the visual arts. Both the Dadaist and surrealist movements of the 1920s and 1930s in Europe were interested in chance and in the unconscious, developing first in response to the ascendancy of bourgeois materialism and then to the emergence of fascism as a political system. Lipska shares this painterly interest in the unconscious, the dream life of images, and in chance—though hers is a *skeptical* surrealism, meaning she calls into question even the surrealists' claim that images are purified of social or political motive, for any *system* of art may give rise to a fascist aesthetic. For Lipska, the poem itself is the site of an accident, an uncalculated intersection between the poet and history.

In the preface to this volume, Lipska recounts the autumn afternoon of an accident: a Volkswagen Passat drives off a bridge into the German Rhine, the waters open to the vehicle, the passengers, and their fate becomes "a dictatorship of the moment." She then asks if a poet has the right to speak on behalf of such a moment. Does the artist have a moral obligation as witness? From which particular vantage point should she speak? Does she look on with the cold, rational eye of death—as in Hannah Arendt's portrait of Adolf Eichmann, or like the rational, "perfectly sane" SS bureaucrat depicted by Thomas Merton? Does she speak as a survivor of the disaster, like Tadeusz Borowski's first-person narrator in his stories in *This Way for the Gas, Ladies and Gentlemen,* or like Primo Levi, who recounts his firsthand experiences as an Auschwitz-Birkenau internee? Or does she dare to speak as a proxy—despite Paul Celan's cautioning, "No one / bears witness / for the witness"—by engaging the empathetic imagination, charging words with their most penetrating meaning? These questions haunt Lipska's poems, particularly the selections from the first three books represented here, *1999, Pet Shops,* and *I.*

To situate Lipska's verse within twentieth-century Polish lyric poetry, it is important to see the work as arising from Poland's distinct encounters with European totalitarianism. The poems are shaped by the legacy of wars, both by Polish cultural memory of the German occupation and the horror of Holocaust atrocities and by the presence of Soviet communism, in particular the two decades of the 1970s and 1980s, during which Lipska matured as a poet. The intersection of history, politics, and the literary arts has typified East European culture for more than two hundred years. In the case of Poland, poetry's break from classicism was defined in great part by a nationalist impulse. Nationalism came to define the romanticism of nineteenth-century Polish poetry, as in the works of Adam Mickiewicz, Juliusz Słowacki, and Zygmunt Krasiński. The role of the Polish poet became one of an *acknowledged* legislator, to reverse Shelley's depiction of British romantic poetry. In Polish lyric poetry, neither does the speaker stand outside time nor does the poem consist of epiphanic moments where time stops and human experience expands. Rather, the Polish lyric becomes the site of intersection between social forces and the individual, primarily because the genre has repeatedly served national political agendas.

The romantic vision informing contemporary Polish lyric poetry is most often enacted via the speaker's ironic stance in relation to history, at least in part as a consequence of modern Polish poets' struggle with totalitarianism. The poems typically address silence, both the censorship that characterizes a totalitarian political culture and the inadequacy of language to articulate the most highly charged human experiences. In this sense, Lipska's poems are contemporary lyrics. But perhaps more important for Lipska, as Susan Gubar has noted, "poetry after Auschwitz displays the ironic friction between the lyric's traditional investment in voicing subjectivity and a history that assaulted not only innumerable sovereign subjects but indeed the very idea of sovereign selfhood" (12). Lipska's poems in particular offer a unique opportunity to contemplate identities (personal, social, national) as constituting both personal and historical forces, and one's own interior life as the site of this intersection—what Lipska might call "the accident" or "spectacle of our lives," which one both participates in and observes as witness.

We open *The New Century* with the poem "December 31, 1999" because it enacts not only the death of a century, a millennium, but also the birth of another: "But the night won't be childless./ Taking by surprise the doubting suicides / and gullible priests, / the New Year's infant / will scream at midnight." And it is also the birthday of Simon Wiesenthal. Thus, this particular New Year's Eve offers an opportunity to penetrate, move beyond, the barrier to the human spirit imposed by the century's genocides. For Lipska, Wiesenthal is a guide to rendering the impossible possible, "a compass drawing square." Not only did he manage to survive internment in Nazi camps at Ostbahn, Janwska, and Mauthausen; more remarkably he lived to avenge victims of the Shoah by assisting in bringing to trial as many as eleven hundred war criminals, including key Nazi military personnel. The particular human voice of the "New Year's infant [who] will scream at midnight" defies the imposed silence of the former century. To launch the volume with this poem is to root the work that follows in the integrity of the individual life, the sovereign self posited against erasure.

Because they offer English-language readers the trajectory of Lipska's thought into the twenty-first century, the poems selected from *1999* and from *Newton's Orange* are the focus of our translation. In these poems in particular, Lipska's relationship to language is richly complex, and in them we see contradictory impulses at work. This dialectic moves between her loss of faith in language's ability to communicate meaning (whether it fails for the social purpose of enabling justice or for the more personal purpose of enabling human empathy and intimacy) and her deep reliance on words as a poet's artistic medium. One stylistic strategy Lipska uses to address this paradox is the stereotypical language of the cliché. The poet recognizes that human communication is essentially derivative, based on rhetorical patterns we inherit, cannot escape, and that render genuine communication of our personal experience impossible. Lipska enjoys rupturing such clichés—colloquialisms or jargon ranging from religious to technological discourse—in order to create a singular, individual voice. For example, in "God Asks" Lipska substitutes *grzech* (sin) for *brzeg* (side or riverbank), which sound nearly identical, as a satiric pun on the Polish idiom for death; rather than "cross over to the other side," the poet writes "cross over to the other sin." Similarly, in "Hannah Arendt" she describes Arendt and Heidegger as "not having regained death" (*śmierci*), rather than employing the typical Polish idiom for "not having regained consciousness." But I believe that Lipska would argue that even in these cases, language fails, for it can offer us little more than a highly idiosyncratic, and perhaps impenetrable, code or the superficiality of stereotypical language. The task of the poet—this tension and struggle between the authentic human voice and rhetoric—is a central theme in Lipska's work and one permeating all the poems included in this volume.

Readers will find resonances of the philosophical and artistic themes infusing *1999* and *Newton's Orange* in selections included from the other four volumes represented here (published by Wydawnictwo Literackie between 2001 and 2007). Ewa Lipska's poems defy categorization. They are unique among those by other East European poets in their use of a surrealistic imagination to enact a subversive, ironic wit in the service of skepticism. Metaphorically, Lipska's poetic oeuvre employs the hermetic methodology of a besieged people: it is buried cultural treasure; it is a system of secrets and revelations; it is a collection of keys. And the work relentlessly engages centuries of social systems (political, economic, scientific, technological, artistic) and their vocabularies to examine the viability of human knowledge and the motivations underlying it. For Lipska, to look forward is to look back, in that each new century is fundamentally no different from the old one, yet it always trembles with the possibility of newness without regard to being doomed in advance. Given the inevitability of human error, greed, and the illusory nature of our perception, Lipska may well be asking, how does one craft a place for love, the consolation of its redemptive power in our lives? The life of Simon Wiesenthal offers one possible response. The poems presented here are most certainly a tribute to Wiesenthal, whose life and work, imbued as they are with a capacity for authentic human connection, signify the complexity of what it has meant to be a survivor of the twentieth century.

Adorno, Theodor W. "Cultural Criticism and Society." In *Prisms,* translated by Samuel Weber and Shierry Weber Nicholsen, 17–34. Cambridge, Mass.: MIT Press, 1981.

———. "Lyric Poetry and Society." In *Critical Theory and Society: A Reader,* edited by Stephen Eric Bronner and Douglas MacKay Kellner, 155–71. New York: Routledge, 1989.

———. "Meditations on Metaphysics." In *Negative Dialectics,* translated by E. B. Ashton, 361–65. New York: Continuum, 1973.

Arendt, Hannah. "Authority in the Twentieth Century." *Review of Politics* 18, no. 4 (1956): 403–17.

———. *Eichmann in Jerusalem: A Report on the Banality of Evil.* New York: Viking Press, 1963.

———. "Introduction." In Walter Benjamin, *Illuminations: Essays and Reflections,* edited by Hannah Arendt, 1–55. New York: Schocken Books, 1968.

Arendt, Hannah, and Martin Heidegger. *Letters, 1925–1975.* Edited by Ursula Ludz. Translated by Andrew Shields. New York: Harcourt, 2004.

Bakhtin, M. M. "Epic and Novel: Toward a Methodology for the Study of the Novel." In *The Dialogic Imagination,* edited by Michael Holquist, translated by Caryl Emerson and Michael Holquist, 3–40. Austin: University of Texas Press, 1981.

Barańczak, Stanisław. "Introduction." In *Spoiling Cannibals' Fun: Polish Poetry of the Last Two Decades of Communist Rule,* translated by Stanisław Barańczak and Clare Cavanagh, 1–13. Evanston, Ill.: Northwestern University Press, 1991.

Benjamin, Walter. "Theses on the Philosophy of History." In *Illuminations: Essays and Reflections,* edited by Hannah Arendt, 253–64. New York: Schocken Books, 1968.

———. "Unpacking My Library." In *Illuminations: Essays and Reflections,* edited by Hannah Arendt, 59–67. New York: Schocken Books, 1968.

Borowski, Tadeusz. *This Way for the Gas, Ladies and Gentlemen.* Translated by Michael Kandel. New York: Penguin Books, 1976.

Carls, Alice-Catherine. "Ewa Lipska: *1999.*" Review. *World Literature Today* 74, no. 1 (2000): 194.

Cavanagh, Clare. "Poetry and History: Poland's Acknowledged Legislators." *Common Knowledge* 11, no. 2 (2005): 185–97.

———. "Postcolonial Poland." *Common Knowledge* 10, no. 1 (2004): 82–92.

Davies, Norman. *Heart of Europe: The Past in Poland's Present.* Oxford, U.K.: Oxford University Press, 2001.

Golb, Norman. "The Dead Sea Scrolls: A New Perspective." *American Scholar* 58, no. 2 (1989): 177–207.

Gubar, Susan. *Poetry After Auschwitz: Remembering What One Never Knew.* Bloomington: Indiana University Press, 2003.

Horkheimer, Max, and Theodor W. Adorno. "The Culture Industry: Enlightenment as Mass Deception." In *Dialectic of Enlightenment,* translated by John Cumming, 120–67. New York: Continuum, 1972.

Kolakowski, Leszek. "The Priest and the Jester." In *Toward a Marxist Humanism: Essays on the Left Today,* translated by Jane Zielonko Peel, 9–37. New York: Grove Press, 1968.

Krall, Hanna. *The Subtenant* and *To Outwit God.* Translated by Jarosław Anders. Evanston, Ill.: Northwestern University Press, 1992.

Levi, Primo. *Survival in Auschwitz: The Nazi Assault on Humanity.* Translated by Stuart Woolf. New York: Simon and Schuster, Touchstone, 1996.

Lipska, Ewa. *Białe truskawki / White Strawberries.* Translated by Barbara Plebanek and Tony Howard. Kraków: Wydawnictwo Literackie, 2000.

———. *Drzazga.* Kraków: Wydawnictwo Literackie, 2006.

———. *Gdzie indziej.* Kraków: Wydawnictwo Literackie, 2005.

———. Interviews by Robin Davidson. Kraków, Poland, January 31, 2004; May 25, 2007.

———. *Ja.* Kraków: Wydawnictwo Literackie, 2003.

———. *1999.* Kraków: Wydawnictwo Literackie, 1999.

———. *Poet? Criminal? Madman?* Translated by Barbara Plebanek and Tony Howard. Boston: Forest Books, 1991.

———. *Pomarańcza Newtona.* Kraków: Wydawnictwo Literackie, 2007.

———. *Sklepy zoologiczne.* Kraków: Wydawnictwo Literackie, 2001.

Merton, Thomas. *Raids on the Unspeakable.* New York: New Directions, 1964.

Miłosz, Czesław. *The History of Polish Literature.* Berkeley: University of California Press, 1983.

Parlej, Piotr. "Zagajewski: Between Romanticism and the Avant-Garde." *Samizdat Magazine* 1 (1998), http://www.samizdateditions.com/issue1/polishpoetry1.htm.

Wolin, Richard. *The Terms of Cultural Criticism: The Frankfurt School, Existentialism, Poststructuralism.* New York: Columbia University Press, 1992.

Zagajewski, Adam. Interview by Robin Davidson. Houston, Texas, April 12, 1997.

Four Notes on Ewa Lipska's Poems

Ewa Elżbieta Nowakowska

ART

Ewa Lipska is never deadly serious about such notions as "inspira-tion," "creation," or "art." She deeply mistrusts *wena*, a Polish term, used mainly in highbrow literature, referring to poetic inspiration or moments of illumination. She ironically traces *wena* back to its Latin origin, *vena*, meaning simply "vein." Lipska asks, "Does anyone still remember that *vena* is only a vessel carrying blood?" Blood is a sym-bol of life, so physiological that eventually it is life as such that pre-vails and art may be dismissed as "an excess of nothing." Since artists mostly suffer from hubris and bravado, art does not matter much, unlike love, which is the most important factor conditioning human life and endowing it with meaning. It may even resist history and bureaucracy, which unscrupulously encroach upon art's territory: no wonder that we may at times find "an unexplained metaphor / in civil registers." Nevertheless, love, "a twig stirred by the wind / is always Number One / and leans toward us."

Lipska claims, "There are no poets. / There is only the inattentive moment," which means that to some extent poetry is an accident, a freak of nature, a wonder. In an interview Lipska admitted: "Poetry should not say too much. It is enough when it sends some signals. Obviously, not to every reader. But I do not want to write for every reader." She is never afraid that her latest book may turn out to be the last: "You may not write poems for many months or years, it makes no difference. The point is you should not lose your ability to experience everyday reality creatively." She also has some witty advice for young poets: in "Watch Your Step" Lipska addresses beginners who send her letters with their unfledged poems in the hope of being praised and promoted, but instead of extolling them, she draws their attention to "the perfect choreography / of emptiness" that emerges whenever you tense "the muscles of words." Artists should constantly be on their guard, aware that the direction may suddenly change and they may head for an abyss.

In one of her later books, *Splinter,* she returns to the theme of a beginning poet who writes to her, his act of creation apparently resembling the labor of a carpenter in a sawmill. It seems that all poets use the raw material of language, compared here to lumber, but the more they write, the less lumber they are left with. Finally they have something like a pencil stub or a splinter, lodged in their memory, "hard to remove / much harder to describe." This metaphor seems an adequate way of rendering the mystery of writing and creating.

In a more recent poem, however, Lipska mentions "rustproof volumes of my poems," which may mean that, according to the poet, art does not corrode and is more permanent. She said in an interview: "Writing poems is a form of living my life. I never expected it to become chronic."

FATE

Fate recurs in Lipska's poetry as a force that mocks us, deprives us of everything or lavishes dubious gifts on us. As human life is just a "brief transit across a planet," our fate, always unpredictable, plays hide-and-seek with us and, being "multidigital," makes up a part of cosmic red tape. In "Helplessness" the protagonist has "been living on borrowed time": the Polish original says that he has received his fate as a gift, which is a Polish idiom. We do not know who the donor of the gift may be: even if it is God, we cannot call him generous, neither is the fate enviable. Moreover, fate itself (when it becomes the donor) never gives anything out of generosity. On the other hand, it is not infallible; in "Anthem of Fog" Lipska writes: "Fate missed an opportunity. / It could have given you a chance. / Then. At four A.M. / Now it's regretful."

BEAUTY

Expressing her distrust of art, Lipska remarks in one of the poems that a beautiful landscape may turn into a novel greater than any work executed by an artist. However, she has not always admired and loved beauty and nature. When in her youth she combated a serious disease and often visited hospitals, her poetry was pervaded with sadness and a fear of beauty: "Beauty used to hurt me more than it does today. When I was standing on a hill overlooking San Francisco at five P.M., I was overcome by nostalgia and the awareness that everything passes away . . . I was taken aback by the *drama* of beauty . . . The world of dying constantly clashed with the world of beauty," recalled Lipska in a press interview. "Now I perceive it in a milder way. Five P.M. has elapsed. There is more and more shadow, beauty is getting older. Beautifully getting older," she added.

TRANSLATION

Lipska is pragmatic in her approach to translation. Whenever I ask her a question related to an ambiguous word in a poem or to one of her numerous puns, for which she has become so famous in Poland, she always says: "Save as much as possible, but remember to give priority to content, not to form. I know English is so different. It is the meaning that matters." Once when I was worried about rendering into English her brilliant metaphor *wysypisko śmierci* (death dump), a modification of the phrase *wysypisko śmieci* (garbage dump) by adding just the letter *r* (*śmieci* thus becoming *śmierci*) and regretted not being able to come up with an adequate counterpart, she remained serene: "The meaning is crucial, not playing with letters."

THE NEW CENTURY

from **1999**

(1999)

December 31, 1999

S. W.

All the poets will write about it.
Even the illiterate ones.
There will be rumors that it is the last.
That after this, comes only metal-plated fear.
A compass drawing square.

But the night won't be childless.
Taking by surprise the doubting suicides
and gullible priests,
the New Year's infant
will scream at midnight.

The sudden hawk of a wind
will bend the willow.
The compass will indicate
there is no other choice.
The usual drill of the hours.

Your birthday. Despite everything.
A compass drawing square.

The Albatross and the Engraver

The engraver's hand grown into the wing.
The victim of a cooling work
with a sentence lodged in the throat
hardening as suddenly as plaster.
In the walled-in coloratura of breathing
the bel canto of the last breath.

It's the same
with all masters.
The cause of the accident
is the hubris of creating.
The haughty arrogance of talent.
The neglect of caution with the knife
as the world's negative
slices in half.

Hannah Arendt

She.
Hannah Arendt
Euro City on the Heidelberg-Hamburg line.
Chronic love rushing
through submissive squares of fields
the lingering infection of Europe
the banality of evil.

He.
Martin Heidegger
the *Führer* of philosophy.

He'd be a train as punctual
as faith is ambiguous.

March. March. The long-distance march.
Fanatical tangles of passing stations.
The *Vaterland*
under fate's open sail.

They.
Hannah Arendt
Martin Heidegger
died
without having regained death.

New volunteers
already stand on the platform,
invoking their baggage.

They carefully unpack ideologies
drowned out by the backhoe of being—
philosophy's foster aunt.

We 1998

Gone is the scattered time
when we played with fire
while cities burned.

We shortened our journeys
by reading books.
The moving scenes outside the window
stuck to the subject of life.

Those who cried that power belongs to the masses
are now seting up devotional shops.
Trysting sites for timid chameleons.

The new generation set in practical landscapes
now has its own country. Civil service. Self-assured beauty.

Maybe it's just the same virus of transience.

The need to resign oneself to crime's vibration
in the goose down of air.

Their hope, indispensable to sleep,
has not yet expired under the statute of limitations
when they are woken at dawn by poetry's attendants
for a duel of words.

They watch us carefully
like classics flying by
whose wings
clap out angels.

When a Great Poet Dies in My Country

When a great poet dies
in my country
an orphaned patrol of pilgrims starts up.

A couplet in the sky.
The manuscript of the setting sun.

The poet is hunted
by greedy critics.
Suspicious patriots.
Skillfully tailored lovers.

The legend
which was seen circling the area
has nothing more to add.

Moreover, an ungodly heat
and a desperate time.

An unexplained metaphor
in civil registers.

The transit of *Saturn*
confirmed by the local press.

And he. Though already without the pulse of his tongue
he's apparently still writing.
Much further from the casino of history.
From truths squandered on those nights
when the full moon of a vowel unmasks us.

The Honor of Tragedy

We sit at a vegetarian dessert
and meddle in everything
nosy prose writers.

Past the third page of the obituaries
a recipe for butter cookies.

Debauched discussions of inspiration.
Of the indecent ease of creating.
Licentious alliteration.

Does anyone still remember
that *vena* is only a vessel
carrying blood.

A pulse in the temples
follows the last sentence.

A herd of banalities wanders
the peat bogs of adjectives.

A landscape endowed with talent
makes for a much better story.

But our tragedy has honor
and toasts all artists, drinking
the ocean's ironic allusion.

God Asks

That you not invoke him. That you not buy and sell him.
That you not hang his grace from political stalls.
That you not use the alibi *Gott mit uns*
for a godless crime.
That you not perform rituals of evil
in his name.
That you not take in vain
the adoration of the shepherds.
That you not shove. Not squander.
Not burn anyone at the stake.

From the charred eye
ran a tear.

Perhaps he will come to you
o, wretched humanity,
as you cross over
to the other sin.

The Smells of Evil

The secret agent of order.
He would like most to sue
the chaos of uncertainty.

He places a teaspoon of obligatory jam
into the mouth of a child.
The assimilated taste
is passed from mouth to mouth.

The univocal believer
has mastered to perfection
the smells of evil.

The valedictorian of the unenlightened star
gazing at the sky of hypocrisy.

Bound, however,
to the black sect of night
when he is haunted
by the widow of good deeds
who treacherously offers him
a sensual coup d'état.

Watch Your Step

You
who write me letters
shamelessly young archers
tensing the muscles of words,
can you see the perfect choreography
of emptiness?

And when this space
gets in your blood.

And when this plain
smooth as a sheet of ice
gets in your blood.

And when this even ease of life
gets in your blood.

Watch your step.
There will be a sudden change of direction.

And when you reach your target
all that will continue
is direction.

Note

I remember him walking away.
He tipped the table, spilling
the overture to our city.

He knew that we die
neither yesterday nor tomorrow.

The snap of cut stems
he bequeathed to his creditors.

He couldn't be late anyway
because the crowd of gawkers was already waiting
asking that we not offer
expressions of admiration.

Love

No explanations. No references.
Footnotes. Entries.
A carousal of silent vines.

Everything depends on
how long we will be always.

Ericsson, Child

We are sick with the century's decline.
Saved only by mountain ranges
of antibiotics
welded with metallic grass.

The valleys are overgrown with noise.
I say something to you.
To you all. To no one.

Your love for me
confesses itself over the phone.
Ever louder, around us,
a staggering
stream.

We connect our child prodigy
to the network.

Ericsson, child,
pray to the satellite.

Because what more can you do
during your brief transit
across a planet. Razed to the earth.

The Holy Order of Tourists

Landscapes doomed in advance to success.
Devotional seacoasts.
A crowd of practicing believers.

For those
who run
into the Church of Santa Maria della Salute
to admire the paintings of Titian and Tintoretto
solemn vows: *vota sollemnia.*

For others
the strict rule of a scorching sin.
The fainting body of the desert
populated with a faithful crowd.

Frightened animals run away
from the monastic jungle.
Vertical space boils
in the holy order of tourists.

John Keats

Destiny lost its mind
when he came into the world.

A dog met on a cliff's secret path
told barefaced lies.

Fate drowned in swamps
bogs quagmires.

Supplies of close friends
were running out.
Love used itself up.

Actually
only tuberculosis
loved him.

Time began
a battue hunt
driving deaf critics
(all trace of them lost)
after his poems.

*Now he is scattered
among a hundred cities,*
W. H. Auden would write of him
in his too-long poem.

Already his third life
coughs in me,
spitting rivals from my lungs.

2001

2001, dear Mrs. Schubert, is not only the beginning
of the new century, but also the number of my imagination.
As you know, for some time now my fiction
has resented my flirting with reality,
consorting with useless time.
I therefore inform you that the dead season is coming,
which, as usual, I am spending
on the short-term list of missing persons.

from PET SHOPS

(2001)

Fashion Craze

We die more and more beautifully
in Gianni Versace's collection.
Elegance is aesthetics' nestling.

We bustle about the churches of fashion
believing that the orange will suit us.

You kiss me in a changing room
Look, it's just Rome's fall in green.

We solve the puzzles of our archetypes.
Translate berets into foreign languages.

Tonight we are invited
to the opening of the Last Judgment.

We enter without tickets.
Today is dead admission.

The New Century

The new century has come as no surprise.
After midnight we already call it by name.

Your dress lies beside the bed.
My suit a pirate flag.

Reports warn us
about the slippery surface of history.

The question of *what comes next*
we send back to the gala.

We speak to each other in fireworks.
A drowsy noun in the mouth.

We subject breakfast to laboratory tests.
314 calories on a white plate.

We're zipped fast
into a lifeproof vest.

Calvin

A slim one. And shy.
Little sleep. Headaches.
He was afraid of fear.

He lived in an age of crime tourism.
Letters of suspects. Arrests. Executions.

A good time for pyromaniacs. During processions
on six sites of meditation
stakes of burning convicts.

Inexhaustible avenues of treason.

The year 1535. In Paris.
His room was meticulously searched.
Papers confiscated. Correspondence.

He's the author of a treatise on *the dream of the soul.*

In Catholics he discerns *Satan's audacity.*
To top it all bubonic plague. Famine.

The year 1541. Return to Geneva.
Mutual provocations.
Fanatical hatred.

Terror yapping in the streets.

Religion doesn't save him. A utopian vision
of eternity.
He weakens. Weakens more and more.

A dry landscape. A red trickle of light.
Echo of evil.

He weakens. Weakens more and more.
He dies.
Converted into sin.

Pet Shops

Pet shops.
The internment camp
from my childhood.

Guinea pigs. Parrots. Canaries.
The sickly scent of captivity.
Sawdust of events.

At home I would spit out depression.
Antigone the cat didn't show up anymore.
A mousetrap from Verdun
and then all the way to Auschwitz.

I didn't know how it would end
when I signed up for life.
A volunteer.

Fog

A fog like Marcel Proust's asthma.
Give me your hand, darling.
White faking navy blue.
There's not even a piano.

Further north
people are like an ice floe.
An heirless breath
circles around our mouths.

At the gas station
we part ways.
The eloquent absence of language.
Give me your hand, darling.

The subscription to time has expired.
Goodbye, darling.
Your city is to the left.
Mine to the right.

Further north
people are like an ice floe.
Your city is called *Omen.*
Mine's called *Nomen.*

Nomen omen is a Latin phrase indicating that the very name of a person or thing is a sign of the character or nature of that person or thing.

Press Enter

Forever and ever Enter
(in the news)

The most state-of-the-art crematorium in Europe.
Berlin Treptow. An Arcadia of mourning.

The holy order of computers with eyes of lusterless crepe.
A web of silence. Only the rustle of artificial leaves.

The afterlife of Pentium.
Immortal memory.

The concurrence of two days in one.

For the deceased a hairdresser. Beauty treatments.
A photographer's studio. Warm blackness.

Antivirus software on guard at each floor.
(Torrential content outside the window.)

A casket on a hard disk.
We lie there in the index of names.

A droplet in the corner of the mouth.
Moisture of dead love.
We were in love when this happened.

Now there's only a file connected to the sky.
A closed database.
An orphaned cloud from the chimney.

Are you sure you want
to begin deleting?

Press Enter

The Accident

The police claimed
that the turn was seeking revenge.
It shrank suddenly. Curved.
An asphalt illusionist.

Poets know this moment
when it's still too soon to scream
but too late to stop the tongue.

On speeding motorcycles
headed straight into the ruin of fog.

from **I**

(2003)

Number One

And so what
that our planet
is bookable.

The moon listed in property records.
The sun included in a notarized deed.

Numbered cities. Mortgaged streets.
Multidigital fate.

New wars
secured
by real estate of the Decalogue.

Exorbitant sums of hope
at public auctions.

And so what
when love
a twig stirred by the wind
is always Number One
and leans toward us.

A Juicer

So many saints
that they block out the heavens.
We'll also buy a plastic Christ.
Holy water which will be absorbed
by the blotting paper of sin.

Unbelieving thoughts
watch us closely.

Love converts us.

A reckless juicer
squeezes shy testimony from us.

Yes.

I

I.
Numerological number one.
Friend to gardeners and painters
I hide my memories
in the chamber of a gun
and return to the exit.

It is the year 2003.
A quiz show is on in the next room.
An excess of nothing.
The neurotic scent of basil.

In the entry hall I hang
my lifeboat back up.

Christoph P.
a photosensitive photographer
takes a picture of me.

The title of this poem in Polish (and of the collection from which it comes) is "Ja," meaning the personal pronoun "I."

No One

I agree to this landscape
which does not exist.

Father is holding a violin.
The children are licking at the sound.

A draft
brushes the rose petals.

Then the war. We lose sight of one another.
Huddled in full sentences, words are in hiding.

An empty room
parked in the twilight
of an old apartment house.

Please leave a message,
says no one.

Home

My nanny crosses
a diagonal of time.

On the table a golden broth.
Textbook examples of letters in English.

With a heavy poem on my heart
I open the door.

Our secrets creak
as we drink cod-liver oil.

My brother
the consul general
smiles in his allotment garden outside Kraków.

In the distance our family home.
A black box. The digression of an accident.

That

We sit with the cat and nanny
on the bus of a photo album.

Rain and sepia outside the window.

The river flows into us.
An undertow of pain.

A pale Jesus in the picture.
The sled propped against the wall.

I am a worshipper of coniferous time
while a devout tawny owl
prays for nanny.

September 11, 2001

Poets spies pious taxpayers
songwriters jewelers
will all be announcing
reports of the crime.

At times even poems. At times even songs.

Jewelers will polish the facts meticulously.
Proper shape. Proper shine.
Catastrophe's precise costume jewelry.

Naturally
everyone will commit themselves to print.

And only my dressmaker
with whom I talk quietly
in satin stitches
says
the world has unraveled.

And the sewing machine
laughs caustically.

from ELSEWHERE

(2005)

Elsewhere

I'd like to live Elsewhere.
In hand-embroidered towns.

To meet those
who are not born into the world.

At last we would be happily alone.
No stop would wait for us.

No arrival. No departure.
Evanescence in a museum.

No wars would fight for us.
No humanity. No army. No weapon.

Tipsy death. It would be fun.
In the library, multivolume time.

Love. A mad chapter.
It would turn the pages of our hearts in a whisper.

From a Distance

From a distance I look at the house
the last story line is running away from.
Mr. Ferek. His wife. His dog.

Nanny in heaven. Stuffing doughnuts with rosehip preserves.
The throat of a rivulet run dry.
Cats scattered.

Bedrooms still engage in conversations.
Ah, yes . . .

A sudden downpour washed
the traces of our mouths away.

Out of the entire spectrum of colors
only the red fur of wayside poppies
is left for me.

Plum Cake

I remove from your face
a crumb of plum cake.
A tiny print of tenderness.

Far from any ideas
I place it on the ancient china of the page.
Let it be recorded forever.

We don't know when
a draft blew everything away.
Someone opened a window. Someone opened a door.

After years
I still visit pastry shops.
I resent your being only an illusion for me.
And even the night cannot guess
when we are together.

Helplessness

The life which he was bequeathed
as grandma used to say
what kind of inheritance is that anyway?

He drags behind him days
he'd rather not have known.
A concentration camp childhood.
Barbed wire toys.

A suitcase from those days
airmailed
is still pretending to be a bird.

He's been living on borrowed time one might say
he's managed to survive.

Till the end he will remain in his own
minority.

Who could make sense of that. Even God
asking for a light in the park's mortgaged darkness
is just helplessness turning to dust.

The Abyss

Sometimes you see plaster
falling from heads.
The facade of reason peeling away.

History again.
Why return to it
since everything is ahead of us anyway.
It is done. It cannot be undone.

I sit beneath any old sky
and listen to what mediocrity has to say.

In prayer books
a bookmark advertising
antiwrinkle fowl.

From every nation *you know it*
murderers can be wrung out.

Monument

A monument. Sympathy on sale.
Memory stoned to death
on which children on a school trip sit
pulling out hunger sandwiches.

A minute's cooing
of lurking pigeons.

The fear of concrete
the kitsch of death
and the loneliness of victims.

Memory

The froth of dandelion puffs. Nanny again.
She still hovers behind me in my poems.
With Sidol she wipes words. Brass door handles.

Be careful on the stairs, put a warm scarf on.

In the mirror a wilderness in a gray coat.
With threadbare sleeves worn out at the road's turns.
A look-alike of your love leaning against the gate.

How can I explain to you
fingerprints on mouths.
Not everything was said.

And why should it be
since there is no longer this language.
No us. No star
which was on duty.

Inattentive Moment

There are no poets.
There is only the inattentive moment.

Wordplay on a busy street.
Just in case
of accidental verse.

from SPLINTER

(2006)

Anthem of Fog

Fate missed an opportunity.
It could have given you a chance.
Then. At four A.M.
Now it's regretful.

And you like a ski jumper
with whom the air fell in love forever.
Higher and higher further and further
from the screaming anthem of the fog.

Splinter

I like you a twenty-year-old poet writes to me.
A beginning carpenter of words.

His letter smells of lumber.
His muse still sleeps in rosewood.

Ambitious noise in a literary sawmill.
Apprentices veneering a gullible tongue.

They cut to size the shy plywood of sentences.
A haiku whittled with a plane.

Problems begin
with a splinter lodged in memory.

It is hard to remove
much harder to describe.

Wood shavings fly. The apple cores of angels.
Dust up to the heavens.

Live Update

Your Live Update has expired.
No program could be run.

Outside the window
an unrequited landscape.
Bonfires of punctuation.

On a death dump
a raven.

Noah

On the day when the sea drowned
Noah buys low-fare *easyJet* tickets.
Airbus A380. Four Rolls-Royce engines.

It's raining. Mankind is shopping at the Metro mall.
Dogs barking from a handy French horn.
Piccolos of birds in the snares of turmoil.

A lack of discipline rigor order.
It's just earthly anarchy.
A dark chaos of clouds
above the runway.

There's going to be a pogrom against the air,
thinks Noah.

That's Why

Sleet at the table.
At the places of mother father grandparents
a frozen memory. A platter of watches.
Glasses with incurable defects in vision.

Silence lags.
A Christmas carol sinks to the floor.
No one calls anyone for help.

That's why I don't like the holidays.

Spinoza

Your house stands. A path with no commentary.
A bird in a tattered black glove
dismisses everything with silence.
Spinoza grinds and polishes the garden (then tuberculosis)
and I die to you with this
last message.

Absence

Your Absence blooms.
Above me circles
a reconnaissance plane with no pilot.

A blender whisks the clouds to a froth.
An epic scent of Cabbage Rose
after which only the preserves are left.

From a bird's-eye view, with a love song.
You entrust me to life
I, you, to the gardens of Eden.

Dead Stop

When in the wee hours
you were stuck at a dead stop
a train whistling along the dark rainbow of a bridge.

Today I just want to tell you
that the bedside lamp from your room
was promoted to star.

from NEWTON'S ORANGE

(2007)

Newton's Orange

1

I marvel at the debut of new political systems.
The casual elegance of Armani.

Pneumonia wrapped in a shawl of grass.
The latest thing in democracy.

A line of red mouths.
Love cheering.

On the catwalk dead models.
Railroad tracks of makeup
smudged by the impressionists.

Now everything has become clearer.
God has admitted
to being only human.

Under the gray
slice of a cloud
a dud bill of exchanges.

On the screen the unimpeded
motion of the centuries.

They already were.
We are now.
You are yet to be.

We are now.

In the place of Eden stands a city.
A cluster of blocks of flats
graze on stony meadows.

A yellow tennis ball
hits its mark at the light's center.

You are yet to be.

We will make room for you
in the orphaned future.

We leave behind a moderately healthy garden.
Caravaggio's *The Supper at Emmaus.*

Take note of the figure
of the innkeeper.
Of rotten apples. Figs. Pomegranates.

They already were.
We are now.
You are yet to be.

2

I open the door to my books.
Leaves fall out.

On this billiard ball of earth
so much has happened.

The novel of humanity swells.
Bloated chapters of streets
by Giorgio de Chirico.
The imagination's tireless engine.

MacHamlet's onstage.
Self-service theater.
"Poor Yorick." Monosodium glutamate.

Witnesses of history
from a nearby fast food joint.
Farewell to Ophelias made of preservatives.
Chips of fear carried by a gust of wind.

3

Everything was supposed to be different. Then
on the bridge you swore on a rainbow. The future
had an eternity's guarantee.

We planned life
bent over a topographical map.
Breath to breath.
Green dust the color of passion.

At this time
an illiterate was already reading *Mein Kampf.*
Sparks sprung up with a scream.

Now everything has become clearer.

God has admitted
to being only human.

On billboards the hunt for miracles.
Jesus del Pozo perfume
flowing into the sea.

I read my lover carefully.
I recall a memory
with its finest details.

A dream did not wait for us.
We forget that
there is no us.

I go out onto the balcony of the city.
The icicles of light evaporate. I breathe.

I invent everything anew
with my eyes fixed on Newton's orange
and on your eyes
which recover
my vision.

Further and Further

I throw kilometers in front of me.
Like dice.
I extend the illusion.

I place trick mirrors along the roadsides.
Mirages of the perennial idea.

Further. Further. Further and further.
I transfer my life
into the accounts of new cities.

I cross Dadaist borders.
Carousels of multilingual nights.

Further and further from the hoarse stagnations.
The motionless truth of experience.
The stillness of a dog.

On passing billboards
I read Polish words as if they were Greek
and laugh out loud.

Further and further
is closer and closer
to me.

Stain

During a security check
at Zürich Airport
I stand in the magnetic gate.

Useless metal detectors.

The rustproof volumes of my poems.
Sheets of expressive steel. Chrome irony.
The jingling tokens of aphorisms
move as slowly as patience.

Terrorist thoughts
don't plot even
a suspicious moment.

We look into each other's eyes
like metal at metal.

What can a machine know
about the puzzle of poetry
that's been solving me
for sixty years now.

On the scanner's screen
it's only
a stain
on the right-hand side.

Newton's Orange:
The Origin

We are now.

We lie in white fire
making use of spare love.

We hunt for continuation.

Beside us there roars a washing machine
of Wagnerian tenors.
The choir of foam spins.

During the prewash
an angel's white socks.
The misty silks of lingerie.
Facts of linen.

Ambitious solar energies are intriguing.
Economical windmills of Don Quixote.
Love's nuclear reactor.

Our country on our mother's side
belongs to the East.

On lowlands the coarse
cloth of a uniform.
A salon on the outskirts.

On our father's side, Europe
and the cosmetic pact.
The smoothing away of wrinkles.

We are at the altitude of Socrates.
We sail across Akhmatova.

Skiers from a chilling one-act play
pass us by.

A double bass plucks at a string.
Strikes a tender chord.

They already were.
We are now.
You are yet to be.

God withdraws evil from an ATM machine.

Newton's orange swings.
There's a slightly sour taste.

Freedom

My country roams through freedom.
Pretends to be Europe.

The streets lie prostrate in crosses.

A pilgrimage of waiters
carries the Holy Button on a collection plate.

Newton's Orange:
Fate

They already were.

A streak of light in a secondhand bookstore.
Breakfast in Troy.

Remains of ambrosia still in the pitchers.
The sheets of lakes.

Uninhabited territories of love
routed by sex.

Ruins of alphabet letters at the opticians'
who used to rule the world.

The illegible twilight of the gods.

They already were.
We are now.
You are yet to be.

We are now.

Agnostics dozing at the edge of faith.

Fate—time's faithful servant—
wipes away the dust after a nuisance of revolutions.

A wind blows. The forest's accordion folds.
Darkness can be heard. Light can be heard.

In the suburban philharmonic hall
polyphonic animation.

Telephone ringtones
by Johann Sebastian Bach.

They already were.
We are now.
You are yet to be.

You are yet to be.

You still do not speak to cities
which pose for love's adrenaline.

We are now.

Fetishists in patriotic wardrobes
sniff fascist lingerie.

In the wheel of history
an axle has broken.

Beauty,
the private property of the landscape,
looks at me
with your eyes.

Someone
as usual
squanders
the confetti of our ashes.

Your my their bad luck
that only sheer chance
·may predict us.

Newton's Orange:
Era

We are now.

Trapped in family cameras.
Film shorts
on the "Culture" channel.

Chaplin. Monroe. Warhol.
Fame sentenced to life.
Bait for daydreamers.

I open the dawn.
The chill of Bergman.

Pink suspenders
of the thawing day.

We are now.

Born with a letter of recommendation
from shrewd genetics.

Love breathes us
when we run
between
columns of dates.

Behind us
panting with the century
trudges
an obese crime.

Why does it happen like that?
Our answer asks.

A stainless steel life
folds like a knife.

In the Poorhouse of Europe

In the poorhouse of Europe
I deliver a laudatory speech
to everyone
staring
at the carnivorous collections
of tropical plants
in the natural history museum.

A draft nudges freedom.
A synthetic diamond.

In 's Hertogenbosch

In 's Hertogenbosch. Ad van Rijsewijk
reads Polish poems.
I leaf through time. I ask: *What country is this?*

A country into which I intrude
like a white-and-red word.

At the Poetry Reading

You know, Ma'am, the only thing I need God for
is death. I'm afraid that once he's gone, only
Edgar Allan Poe will be left. I feel the dampness
of his words. The mold of deaf evenings. A zigzag creeping
in the dark. Phantoms of mutilated memory. In my dreams
I hear sirens' voices. That is why . . . What
do you do with your fear when you are not afraid?
Where are you waiting out your life? Sometimes
a vision appears, but it pierces me . . . "Follow it,"
—I say—"It's just another kind of freedom."

Newton's Orange:
Infinity

They already were.

They fight a losing battle of dates.
Blurred. Against a background of surly clouds.

In the Hollywood movie theater
a train of abandoned seats whistles.

The remains of films
still breathe through the screen's lips.

"But Venice for me is so much like
the graveyard of happiness that I haven't
the strength to return"—wrote Marcel Proust.

We are now.

In love's globalization
we succumb to sensuous market forces.
Speculative fireworks.

The corrupt bed linens of Shakespeare
in the national theater.

A city of muscular stadiums
clings to us.

A pirated copy of prosperity.

The penitence of a wilted rose
still means nothing to us.

Arrhythmia of infinity.
Gigabytes of memory.

At dawn
a bigoted breeze shivers.

Norton AntiVirus software
scans our lungs.

All around
the broken glass of frost.

You are yet to be.

On a balcony a woman
a cloud resembling a kiss.

New Year's Eve night is trembling.

The twenty-second century.
The twenty-third century.
The twenty-fourth century.

We are connected
by a dye works of sunrises and sunsets.
A polishing shop of magic, words, and fire.

They divide us forever.

God May Prefer Doughnuts

God may prefer doughnuts.
What are our sins to him.

Still the same commedia dell'arte.
Shameless banality. Unpaired love.
Incestuous dreams.

God may prefer doughnuts.

What's it to him, one more betrayal
worth sinning for?
A burning sea of paraffin?

God may prefer doughnuts.

Unbelieving sleds
stall for time
on innocent snow.

A Door Handle

In the sun's brass
it looks like a young
Greta Garbo.

It contains
the travel itinerary
of our hands.

Confidential
it pushes to
the whispers of studies.

During
family quarrels
it slams the voices shut.

Gilded with ambition
it has its style.

Sometimes it falls.
Like deafening silence.

It despises
a rusty padlock.
Confidant of our
sinful thoughts.

At the sight of it
it spits out the key.

Newton's Orange:
Gravity

I meet it
in the city's old market square.
Maybe ancient Rome.

It wears
the sarcastic color
of a failed life.

It sneers at the seconds.
Sunflower seeds.

In its military memory
it retains the changing of the guard.

It presses its ear to the damp ground.
The ticking pulse of the approaching clock hands.

When it lies down
under an absentminded tree
a human
falls on it.